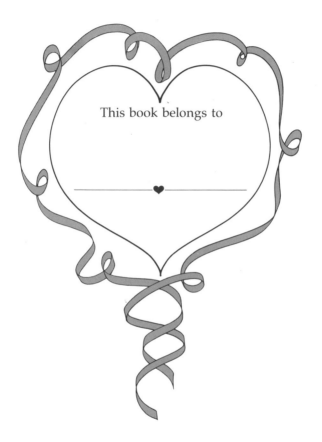

This book belongs to

_____ ♥ _____

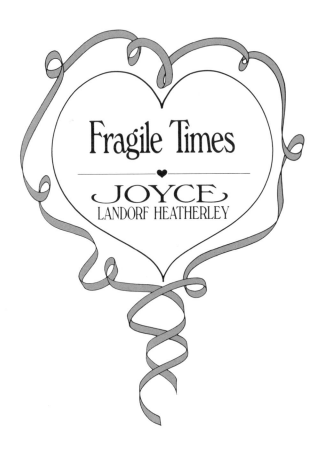

Fragile Times

♥

JOYCE
LANDORF HEATHERLEY

BALCONY PUBLISHING

SALADO, TX 76571

Joyce Landorf Heatherley's selections in this book are favorites from her column, "I've
Been Thinking," which she wrote over a period of years for *Power for Living*.
Printed in the United States of America.

Balcony Publishing
Salado, TX 76571

This book is
lovingly dedicated to
my sister Marilyn
and
my brother Cliff.

Dear Lord,
All around me I see brokenness, and I am aware
of the fragility of life.
There is a child's delicate trust and sense of wonder, which can
be trampled and broken so easily.
There is a teenager's sense of self-worth, which can be shattered
completely by a word or simply by a disapproving look.
There is a family's unit of love, respect, and closeness, which
can be marred by criticism or misunderstandings, dividing
family members into torn and fragmented individuals.
There is a marriage we all thought was so whole and sturdy,
which can splinter into pieces before our eyes.
There is an old man, a young boy, and a middle-aged woman
all suffering from the crushing effects of broken relationships,
which can render their emotions, making them
dangerously frail.
Oh, dear Lord, be the glue that holds fragmented hearts,
broken spirits, and torn minds together. Keep all of us ever
mindful of Your Words:
"I am leaving you with a gift—peace of mind and heart! And
the peace I give isn't fragile like the peace the world gives. So
don't be troubled or afraid" (John 16:33, author's paraphrase).
Thank you, Lord, for those comforting and healing words,
because these are very fragile times and sometimes
I am very afraid.

JOYCE LANDORF HEATHERLEY

♥

I TELL YOU THIS IN CHRISTIAN LOVE

My hair has always been my own personal Waterloo. People who know me find it all very humorous that I can cook, sew, quilt, hook rugs, do yarn pictures, and play the piano, but lose all my manual dexterity when I try to comb my hair. I don't find their teasing one bit funny.

Once, due to a busy schedule before a musical concert, I was rushed into fixing my own hair. After the concert I was really tired, drained of strength, and my mind was fried mush, but I managed to stand and talk with people.

Then *she* stood before me.

"My dear," she began, and by her tone I knew I was going to get it. I braced myself for the next words, which I heard in my head before she said them, "I tell you this in Christian love." Since those words are hardly ever followed by "I love you," I knew what was coming and waited for her critical observations.

She didn't disappoint me. "How long have you been wearing your hair like that?" she asked, shaking her head and pointing at my bedraggled hairdo.

"About three days," I answered.

"Well," she said, "while you were singing, the Lord told me you shouldn't wear it like that; you must definitely change it."

The first reaction I felt was not entirely spiritual, for I would have gladly taken a poke at the old darling without batting an eyelash. But that very week the Lord had been dealing with me about my responsibility to love others—even the annoying ones. Especially the annoying ones.

I prayed silently, "Lord, it's simply not possible to love this lady, much less try to be gracious to her. I'm tired, and she's meddling in my private business. I hate her sweet smile." I wonder which little ole lady said, "I tell you this in Christian love," to David before he wrote, "Restore unto me the joy of Thy salvation" (Psalm 51:12, KJV).

Though my prayer was quick and casual, the Lord seemed to hear and understand, because suddenly I really saw her. She was in her 70s and, I noticed, wearing a badly combed wig! Somehow it had slipped and was actually sitting sideways on her head. The picture of her with her lopsided wig telling me to change my hair struck me as a bit amusing, and considerably restored the "joy of my salvation."

I thanked her for her comments, promised to do something about my hair, and went away giggling.

♥ *Thank You, Lord. I really don't want my attitude to be as unmanageable as my hair.*

♥

BEAUTY SECRET

Yesterday I saw a beautiful woman. Her inner glow was quiet, like a small yellow buttercup; but that same inner glow was loud enough to sound like an explosion in a dynamite factory.

I watched as she talked with other people, how she kept eye contact, how she laughed, how she hugged, how she listened, how she stood; even her body language showing how she cared so much. Then I realized her stunning beauty had a lot to do with a spiritual quality deep within her.

Oh, I don't mean a pious, phoney kind of spirituality. I mean a warm, loving, and tender spirituality. There was nothing hypocritical about her spirituality. It was an honest, sincere, and approachable spirituality.

Yesterday I saw a beautiful woman, and I thought, "No wonder no one can adequately define beauty. It's a fragrance, a God-given ambiance." In each smile she gave, each word she spoke, and even each tear she shed, I saw God. I cannot put my finger on it exactly, but somehow God shines in and through her face.

The rarest thing though, is that she doesn't clobber me with her spirituality. She doesn't throw it up to me about how she gets up early to pray and read the Scriptures each morning. She doesn't tell me who she is fasting for this week or even that she is fasting, yet I think she is.

She didn't leave one single mark of identification on the cupcakes left on my doorstep two days ago, yet I'm sure she brought them. Nor did she ask me later if I enjoyed those cupcakes.

No, when I saw her yesterday, she didn't drive the steamroller of her spiritual achievements over my soul to demand recognition or reward from me.

She is a woman who has taken the words of Jesus seriously and made them her lifestyle. Her gifts to others, spiritual or material, are so nourishing and refreshing. I'm sure she has taken very much to heart our Lord's words:

"Take care! Don't do your good deeds publicly, to be admired, for then you will lose the reward from your Father in heaven. But when you do a kindness to someone, do it secretly—don't tell your left hand what your right hand is doing. And your Father who knows all secrets will reward you" (Matthew 6:1, 3–4).

♥ *Dear Lord, yesterday I saw a beautiful woman and surely You are rewarding her. I just want You to know that as I stood beside her, the essence of her inner spirituality was incredibly fragrant. Thank You, God.*

♥

SIX MONTHS LATER

Both women lost their husbands after 26 years of marriage.

This morning I listened to Ruth (that's not her real name) as she told me about her devastating loss. Her husband died six months ago. "I'm cut in half," she says as she weeps.

Years of sharing everything from thoughts and ideas to toothpaste and the morning newspaper came to a grinding halt for her. She's breaking old patterns, learning to walk and breathe on her own—an adjustment that she neither wanted nor can effortlessly accomplish.

This afternoon's mail brought a letter from Lois (not her real name either). She wrote of her irreparable loss and, like Ruth, she lost her husband six months ago.

She writes that one morning she got up, went out to the kitchen, and found a note propped up against the coffee pot. It read: *Dear Lois, I am leaving you. I will not be back. Sorry. Bill.*

Except for his signature on the divorce papers, she has not seen him since. She never dreamed this could happen to them.

O Lord,
Two women have lost their husbands.
I do not understand the "whys" of either loss.
I find I am gentle, sympathetic, understanding,
and willing to bake cookies for one.
But for the other—
What can I say? What do I do?
She is half a person too, Lord.
Only it's hard to explain her loss to other couples,
relatives, especially the children.

O Lord,
Both of these women are grieving.
Give me a gentle compassion for them.
Not sticky sweet pity, but an open mind and a
listening heart.
Help me not to prejudge the situation
or hold myself up as a paragon of spiritual
righteousness.
Breathe the right words for both women into my
uncomprehending heart,
for I don't know any brilliant, all-
encompassing, and glorious answers.
Their needs, Lord, stir my abilities to listen,
to care, and to comfort.

♥ *I bring both women to You and thank You in advance for the healing which they both so desperately need.*

♥

BACK TO SCHOOL

I've reluctantly signed up for a new course in the school of life. I didn't ask to take the class; I was suddenly pressured into it. What I thought would take a few weeks has turned into a full semester. I've joined a host of others who must study first-hand the problems of prolonged physical pain.

The class sessions are a little irregular. Sometimes class begins at two o'clock in the morning, calling me sharply and noisily out of a deep sleep. Other times it slowly interrupts a friend's afternoon conversation. But if its hours are irregular, its message is not. Consistent pain takes few recesses.

On the days when class is definitely in session, I read "You are a poor specimen if you can't stand the pressure of adversity" (Proverbs 24:10).

I thought, "O Lord, I don't want to be a poor specimen, but I'm weary and the pressures of pain are so constant."

The course is teaching me that pain is monstrously conceited. Pain stamps its foot and demands all my attention. It's hard to decide if I should have baked or mashed potatoes for dinner because pain holds my mind all wadded up in its tightly closed fist.

Pain also teaches the waiting game. Wait for doctor's appointments. Wait for test results. Wait for the medicine to take effect. Wait to see if a new procedure will correct or change the problem.

On the day of this writing, my teacher gave an exam on patience. I passed—but not because I was smart and had graduated to some upperclassman level of maturity. Rather, because I went back to the text, found the right answer, and wrote it down: "We are pressed on every side by troubles, but not crushed and broken. We are perplexed because we don't know why things happen as they do, but we don't give up and quit. We are hunted down, but God never abandons us. We get knocked down, but we get up and keep going" (2 Corinthians 4:8–9).

I don't know how long school will be in session. I'm still in class. I don't like it, but what I do know is that God is in control. I also know the virtue of hanging on, pressing forward, and running the race. I will not give up or quit. I am God's child, but that does not mean I can skip or cut the classes on pain, so . . .

♥ *I thank You, Lord, for whatever this class will be teaching. It's interesting to be this old and back in school again.*

The semester is long, and I'm tired. But Your loving arms of strength are longer. Help me keep that in mind until I graduate.

♥

NOTHING CAN SEPARATE

*I am convinced that nothing can ever separate us from His love.
Death can't, and life can't. The angels won't, and all the powers of hell
itself cannot keep God's love away. Our fears for today, our worries
about tomorrow, or where we are—high above the sky, or in the deep-
est ocean—nothing will ever be able to separate us from the love of God
demonstrated by our Lord Jesus Christ when He died for us (Romans
8:38–39).*

As a musician, I'm well aware of how very precious my
piano is to me. For many years I dreamed of owning a really
great one. Finally, when I could afford it, my dream came true
and I got a used Steinway grand piano. It is still in my living
room today and although it developed a crack in its sounding
board, I love it and lovingly care for it. I still play it almost
every day, keep it tuned, and even dust it regularly.

There is a story about the great violinist, Isaac Stern, who
once took his beloved instrument to a shop for some minor
repairs. The shop owner invited Mr. Stern back to the work-
room to watch as the craftsman fixed the broken part. The

famous violinist is reported to have said, "Oh, no thank you, I'll just sit out here and wait until the operation is finished."

I smiled when I heard that story because I know how attached I am to my piano. I could understand Mr. Stern wanting to be close to his violin, but I could also understand the loving attachment he had to the instrument and his being unable to watch the "surgery."

How very much we Christians are like the violin to the concert master in our relationship with the Lord: God, the Master, and we, His instruments. Only in our case the Lord made us and fashioned us out of nothing. Then He picked us up and, by touching the strings of our lives, brought forth our own original and fantastic music. Music out of sin and chaos, music out of confusion and fear. Music, glorious music.

God's love for us, His instruments, is so strong He will not be separated from us. And unlike Mr. Stern, He not only watches the surgery in our lives, but handles the healing as well. Nothing stops Him from loving.

Paul's wise, joyous words were like a song to me this morning. "Has God deserted us?" the apostle asks. Then the answer comes ringing back again and again. "No! Nothing can separate us from His love!"

On us, His instruments, God plays a song unending. On us, He pours out His inexhaustible source of love, and we in turn will never be separated from it.

♥ *Lord, truly let me be Your usable instrument. I do so want to sing Your songs.*

♥

THE MOTHER-IN-LAW TRAP

If you throw the word *mother-in-law* to a group of people you get the best, sure-fire, break-the-ice game going in the world. Everyone has something to say about his or her mother-in-law.

Unfortunately our society has stereotyped the mother-in-law as meddlesome, destructive, and interfering. Yet for every bad mother-in-law I hear about, I know three or four who are just marvelous.

The reason I've been thinking, studying, and observing mothers-in-law lately is that in less than three months of this writing I'm going to be one. In order to prepare for the event and not to fall into any preset traps, I asked the Lord to teach me all He can about being the very best of mothers-in-law.

I went back to the Book of Ruth. Now *there* was one terrific mother-in-law story and after reading the story again, I was impressed once again of how very strong Naomi and Ruth's friendship was. I want that kind of a loving, secure friendship between my daughter-in-law and me. I have to believe that Naomi and Ruth's relationship didn't "just happen" or "just keep going on its own," but that both women nurtured and meticulously cared for each other.

Next, I was reminded of a "guideline" verse for the years out ahead when I'm mother-in-lawing. I need to remember it, repeat it and apply it daily. It is simple, yet profound. "Be kind to each other, tenderhearted, forgiving one another, just as God has forgiven you because you belong to Christ" (Ephesians 4:32).

Finally, the Lord had me take a good long look at my son, Rick, and my about-to-be daughter, Teresa. It was as if the Lord showed me an instant replay of the 20 years since Rick's birth and how over the years God's hand had guided my son. And then, when I saw the two of them together, I felt that God had Teresa in mind all along. She's wonderful.

I know that the matrimonial road ahead will not be magically smooth. They will have their share of pain and years filled with *more* education. (He is thinking pre-med and she is halfway toward a teaching degree.) Their financial and material cupboards will be quite bare for a long time, but the Lord assures me that they are rich in His love, power, and wisdom.

My responsibility as a mother-in-law boils down to three lovely things:

1. I will lift them in prayer to the throne of God daily.
2. I will be available to them when they need me.
3. I will accept them as they are. God made them and they are His children.

If you see any tears glistening in my eyes the night of their wedding, they will only be tears of joy.

♥ *In fact, I have so much of the Lord's deep settled peace about letting my son go, I think I'll help him pack.*

♥

THEY NEED A MIRACLE

The first rule of being a member of the sanctuary choir was written in red letters. *No talking or passing notes in choir.* So I was a little more than disturbed about the note I could see being slipped from person to person down the front row of choir one Sunday morning. When it reached me, I was even more chagrined because *my* name was on the outside. Hoping that Rollie, our director, didn't see, I opened it to read:

"See the couple on the fifth row in the west auditorium aisle seats? He has on a navy blue suit with a pale blue shirt and she is dressed in lavender."

I looked out over the audience, counted rows, found the blue shirt, and saw a handsome but terribly solemn couple. Then I read on:

"Their marriage is over. Pray for them—they need a miracle." The note was unsigned.

I began to concentrate on loving and praying for this couple who "needed a miracle." Both of them sat attentively facing the pastor; but an expression, smile, or nod never altered their faces as they played the game of "let's pretend we are in church."

As I sat there praying that morning, two things Jesus said were very clearly established in my mind:

1. Jesus asked us to love one another (John 15:12). He did not confine it to people we know and love, but to "one another."

2. Jesus said that with God nothing is impossible (Matthew 19:26).

After I'd committed the troubled-looking couple to God, I began to wonder about the people seated behind them and to the right of them. Do those people need a miracle too? It seemed to me that I'd wasted some prime "praying time" during my many years of sitting in the choir loft. I decided to change that.

The next Sunday during processionals, offering, and other breaks, I searched the congregation for people needing miracles. Prayerfully I asked the Lord which ones were in the most pain and the most need. It's been a rich experience, and praying for others has produced some real growth in my own life.

I never knew what happened to the couple I prayed for that day. They returned for the next three Sundays, but I've never seen them since. I've wondered if they got their much needed miracle. Only the Lord knows just where those two unhappy people are today. I've entrusted them, wherever they are, into His safe keeping.

♥ *Lord, in the meantime, I've picked out an older couple who sit off to my right and three junior-high girls in the balcony. Please give them their seemingly "impossible" miracle for whatever they might need.*

♥

DAD'S HAND

For three winters and summers of my life, my father pastored a church in Owen Sound, Ontario. My memory bank is stuffed with warm recollections of those years.

Of course, when you're only eight years old you see everything larger than life. The summers and the flowers were brighter, bigger, and better than any place in the world. The Georgian Bay water was bluer than any blue had a right to be. The winters were snowier and prettier than any Christmas card ever depicted.

Sometimes after the Canadian winter was firmly set in, we walked to church on Sundays; instead of driving along the river and crossing the bridge, we'd walk across the river on ice.

The first time we did it in December both frightened and excited me. My eager, joyous jumping up and down was instantly squashed the moment my dad and I stepped off the bottom step of the ladder along side the pier and took our first sliding steps onto the ice. Dark rings of slushy ice and water surrounded the big ships on either side of the river. Where we stood seemed safe enough, with thick, firm white ice underfoot. But the terrible blackness around those ships terrified me.

I would never have crossed the frozen path if my father, in loving confidence, had not said, "Joyce, take my hand and walk with me. If you stay right by me, you'll be all right."

And so, hesitantly, I put my little red mitten in his big brown leather glove and we began what looked to me to be a daring journey. But there was something so sure, so confident in my father's strides and manner that almost immediately I lost my terror and the walk turned into a wonderful adventure.

I remember doing a lot of sliding and twirling, pretending I was Sonja Henie, the famous ice skating queen. How bold and brave I was! How joyous and free I acted—all because Daddy held my hand.

Today, I discovered something dark and forbidding in my life and with that sudden jolt of recognition, I understand that I need to reach up and take my heavenly Father's hand. The dark thing still scares me a bit, but my hand is safe inside a larger one.

My heavenly Father is not discouraged. He is not afraid. He is to be trusted. He will not shove me into the dark waters that are icy and over my head. God walks firmly, confidently, and so can I.

I am happy even in the presence of dark things, for my trembling fingers are safely enclosed in His steady hand.

♥ *Lord, thank you for these enduring words: "He fills me with strength and protects me wherever I go" (Psalm 18:32).*

♥

WHY THE HURT, LORD?

It's been many years since David, my infant son, died. You'd think I'd be completely over his death by now, wouldn't you?

One day in the park, when I saw a blond, blue-eyed boy about eight years old trying to get his kite aloft, I remembered David and the hurt was fresh and painful.

He was with me for only a brief flash in time. And I'm aware that my grief is not nearly as deep as a mother's who has 15 or 20 years of memories with a child before he or she is taken. Yet I think any bereaved mother will always yearn and miss the little one that slipped away.

I've been thinking and wondering about the *whys* of our yesterdays' hurts, and I've come up with three ideas.

Maybe one of the best reasons God allows us to remember a pinprick of grief from time to time has to do with His developing a new *awareness and sensitivity to others.*

Losing David gave me unique and different insights in regards to my son, Rick, and daughter, Laurie. It seemed to put a new light on them, and somehow my ability to appreciate them heightened and deepened.

Another reason God allows the hurt seems to be in connection with the word *empathy.*

Having walked in the shadows of death's valley has enabled me to reach out to friends in their times of grief. I can silently and wordlessly cross the bridge of love toward them. I don't need to worry about what I'll say for we are silently bonded together. A hug or a look shows our compassion.

One more reason for the heartache to linger concerns my *understanding* of the grieving process.

Yesterday in the park, when I saw the boy, I asked the *why* of David's going for the hundredth time and patiently, for the hundredth time, God answered.

"My child, stop asking, 'Why did You do that, Lord?' and ask instead, 'What do You want me to learn from this?' I want to teach you many things. Death is a vital part of life. I've allowed you to experience this sorrow to refine your living. You are My child; I am in control, even in David's death. I will continue to direct your path so trust Me, dear child."

♥ *It's been many years since I had my one fleeting glimpse of David's precious face and even more years since that day I saw the boy in the park, but the Lord has been and is faithful—even in the sorrow of this mother's heart.*

♥

IT DOESN'T JUST HAPPEN

It's been quite a year! *Motherhood* has been exploding all around me!

The dog of the neighbors across the street recently gave birth to 10, count 'em, 10 puppies. And Laurie, as she dashed out the front door, startled a brown sparrow off her nest under our roof eaves. Then a friend's cat we were taking care of gave birth to four kittens in one of our closets.

The day Laurie and I watched that cat have her kittens, I was struck by the orderly, tidy procedure she followed. Though it was her first litter, the cat was a study in motherhood as she did whatever had to be done at just the right moment—even though she'd never done it before.

A coincidence? Hardly. I'm sure she waited for her God-given instincts to direct her activities. She did cry out in pain each time a kitten was born, but she seemed to recover quickly and resumed her birth-giving duties.

I kept thinking of the wonder of it all. Who told her to find a cramped, tiny place in a closet so she could push against the wall when she needed leverage? Who taught her the Lamaze method of taking short, panting breaths? Who instructed her about the need to cut the umbilical cord, or to dispose of the placenta, or to meticulously clean each kitten?

I guess what I'm thinking is, after I watched this darling calico-colored mother, it would be difficult to buy an atheistic way of believing. To suggest that all I saw just happens without divine planning seems a little farfetched. In fact, I think it probably takes more faith to be an atheist than it does to believe in God.

My mind can grasp the idea that God created life far better than it can accept that something plus something accidentally crashed together and created this amazing world and even more amazing creatures.

I believe God *did* create and is in control of all the universe. We didn't just happen. No, it had to be planned by a Supreme Being with an awesome creative ability.

"The heavens declare the glory of God; and the firmament sheweth His handywork" (Psalm 19:1, KJV).

Not only do the heavens declare God's glory, but the little living things, like the calico cat and her kittens, declare it as well. How wonderful God is!

Just before writing this, I found out that my son, Rick, and daughter-in-law, Teresa, will be having their first baby. Great! I'll be a grandmother for the first time.

My grandchild's birth will give me another opportunity to observe, firsthand, God's creative abilities.

No, motherhood doesn't just happen. It's a part of God's wonderful plan for us.

♥ *You made all the delicate, inner parts of my body, and knit them together in my mother's womb . . . You were there while I was being formed in utter seclusion! You saw me before I was born and scheduled each day of my life before I began to breathe. Every day was recorded in your Book! (Psalm 139:13, 15–16).*

♥

THE FOURTH 'R'

I vividly remember Laurie's first days at kindergarten, even if it was many years ago. I also will never forget those weeks in August preceding her "big day" before she finally got to go to school.

Before dawn that first day of school, she yanked the covers from off my neck and impatiently pulled me out of bed. She was fully dressed and ready to *go*. I'd never seen such enthusiasm.

Walking to school, we made a strange sight. Laurie ran ahead, then would come back and drag me by the hand, all the time yelling various admonishments like, "Hurry up, please, Mother!" I noticed many other kids were hanging back or hiding behind their mother's skirts or pant legs, crying and walking stiffly as if their own legs were made of wood. I, on the other hand, barely got kissed goodby before Laurie disappeared into Miss Alice's kindergarten classroom.

Later, I asked my breathless daughter (she had run all the way home), "How did it go?"

"Oh, I really like school!" she pronounced.

I was going to ask her what her teacher said, but Laurie was well launched into her report.

"... And Miss Alice said we're going to learn the *four* Rs."

Now I'd heard of three Rs but not four—so I held up four fingers and questioned her with my look.

"Yes, four Rs," she said, "reading, 'riting, 'rithmatic, and right lines."

"That fourth one sounds special, Laurie. Is it?" I asked.

"Oh, yes. It's the most important 'R' there is," she replied.

"How does it work?"

"Well," her look grew confidential and serious, "it's very important to do what Miss Alice tells you, and when she says 'line up,' she means it. But you have to pay attention, because you might stand in the wrong line."

"That's bad?" I asked.

"That's terrible," she said emphatically. "When Miss Alice says line up, you have to be in the right line or you get into big trouble."

About that time our cat Tabby came in, and the two of them had a joyous reunion. Our talk had ended, but my thoughts lingered as I went into the kitchen.

While I made dinner, I thought about the right lines. At home it's up to parents to lay down the "right lines" for our children.

The psalmist wrote, "Show me Your ways, O Lord; teach me Your paths" (Psalm 25:4, Amp.).

I held up those "right lines" and silently asked for God's blessings on my children.

My thoughts were interrupted by the sound of Laurie's voice, "Know why it's really important to get into the right lines, Mom?"

"Tell me," I said, though I knew she would.

"Well, today, Billy wasn't paying attention to Miss Alice and he ended up with the girls in the line that went to our bathroom!"

Ah yes. The four Rs. Thank You, Lord, for the lesson that day, because after all those years, You did lead Laurie into Thy paths and the right lines."

♥ *Happy are those who are strong in the Lord, who want above all else to follow Your steps . . . No good thing will be withheld from those who walk His paths (Psalm 84:5).*

♥

I FEEL SAFE

When Laurie turned 14, she went from sweet to sour overnight. I was grateful that her adolescent rebellion wasn't like that of many of her peers—girls who turned to drugs, alcohol, or ran away. No, with Laurie, she simply stayed home and gave us all fits!

She *hated* everything I wore. Each new skin eruption on her face was treated as a national disaster. She just *knew* she was ugly, repulsive, and hopeless in personality and inner character.

Since she was a perfectly darling girl and I knew I was a "perfectly darling" mother, I had no idea what had hit me or the foggiest notion of how to cope with a teenage daughter.

A few months before Laurie's 16th birthday, I insisted that she go on an Easter choir tour. She was furious with me, but since I gave her no choice, she went (grumbling all the way). It was one of those times my instincts told me that making her go on that tour was right. I slipped a note into her suitcase: "We love you and we are praying for you."

While on the tour, Laurie sent this postcard to her surprised mother: "Thanks so much for the note I found in my suitcase. If ever I needed you to pray for me, it's *got* to be now. I'm scared to sing tonight because there are so many things about God I'm not sure of. Maybe I haven't really taken God down from my 'shelf.' I guess He can be real."

Toward the end of the tour, in many different ways, the Lord became real to her. I knew *something* had happened because she came in the front door, smelled my dinner cooking and said, "Mmmmm, what smells so good, Mom?" The shock was almost too great for me to answer.

A month later I found this note on our bed:

Mom,

This was a year I made 'being parents' very hard for you. I'm sorry for all the hurt I have caused. I have finally realized how much you both mean to me and how much I really love you.

I guess you can say I'm asking for forgiveness. I have asked God for forgiveness, but yet inside I don't feel forgiven. I realize I have to ask you for forgiveness so I can forgive myself and make God's forgiveness complete.

I still am unable to share with you the feelings and emotions I had on the tour or all the feelings of the last four months, but please be patient with me. Sometime I will be able to put the feelings into words.

Mom, I'm glad to be home again. I feel safe.

I share this with you parents who are terribly sure your children will never make it. Laurie is now a grown-up woman, wife, and mother—still learning, still growing, and still beautiful!

♥ *Dear Lord, I will, with your mercy and peace, always keep the porch light on for that one child who may be trying to find his or her way home.*

♥

TEENAGE MEMO

If there is one thing rougher than raising a teenager, it's being one.

Every mistake we parents make usually comes up to hit us head-on during our children's teen years. Even for parents who have done almost everything right, their teenagers can still drop out, rebel, or refute everything they have been taught or believe in.

Most authorities agree that the best advice for parents or teen leaders is to try to see life as teenagers see it.

Recently I saw a list of reminders from a teenager to his parents. It was anonymous, and I suspect it was written by an adult. However, here are a few of the suggestions. They are very real, very down to earth, and they may help you see life from a teenager's viewpoint.

1. Don't spoil me. I know I shouldn't have all that I ask for. I'm really testing you.

2. Don't be afraid to be firm with me. I can respect your firmness if it's fair.

3. Don't let me form bad habits. You may see them early, so tell me. I may not like to be told—but tell me.

4. Don't correct or embarrass me in front of other people.

5. Don't protect me from the consequences of my behavior. I need to learn the painful way sometimes.

6. Don't forget that while I'm growing I cannot explain myself too well. The words I yell may not be what I really mean. You may have to listen from your heart—not your ears.

7. Don't be inconsistent. It really confuses me and disturbs my faith in you.

8. Don't tell me my fears are silly. They are all too terribly real.

9. Don't put me off when I ask what seems to be a dumb question. If you don't answer me, I'll seek answers elsewhere.

10. Don't think you are too spiritual or mature to apologize to me. An honest apology makes me feel surprisingly warm toward you.

11. Don't forget that I love experimenting and changing my mind. Please put up with each phase. I need to work things out.

12. Don't forget you are responsible for my Christian training. Please continue to show God to me by the way you live—not by what you preach.

I pray these 12 rules will give you some extra insights into coping with the teenagers you're concerned about.

♥ *Dear Lord, don't ever underestimate the incredible power of prayer for my children. After all, down here, I may be their only SAFE place of refuge.*

♥

IN CHARGE OF CHOICES

She flung herself through the front door. "I told them *my* mother wouldn't let me go see it!" she shouted angrily at me.

O dear Lord, she's still so young, this beautiful daughter of mine.
I guess about all I know is that someday I'll have to answer to You about her.
I can't let her go to this particular movie, Lord—it's not a family film. It's
    more. Much more. Terribly more.
I'd love to please her.
I'd like to give in, even though I've said no.
I love her so.
I'd like to grant her whatever her dear little heart wants.
But can I and still answer to You?

In five more years we will reach our 20-year mark together.
Then she'll be doing the choosing on her own.
She'll be making the decisions.
But for now; O Lord,
Keep me strong while I'm "in charge of choices."
Help me not to become so stiff and rigid
That I snap with brittleness,

Not so soft that I bend in any direction like a wet noodle,
But keep me supple and pliable,
Able always to move in Your direction.
Lord, I can't drag our daughter through Your gates by her hair.
Guide me in providing the best decisions,
So I can post all the right road signs along the way.

As to this film . . . O Lord,
I think it's far too heavy for her to carry.
Right now at this age, she needs to grow
And to be stronger before she tries out her carrying ability.
She's in her room now,
Still mad at me I expect,
But nevertheless You have put me "in charge of choices."

You were right about me,
Darling daughter.
I won't let you go see *that* movie.
But, then,
You already knew that and I think that in your heart of hearts,
You were counting on it.

♥ *Dear Lord, how come when I tell my children "no" they don't respond with a burst of applause for dear old Mom? Sorta like me, huh? Especially when You say "No." Forgive me Lord. Help me to trust you in the "no"s as well as the "yes"es.*

♥

FED UP WITH CHRISTIANS?

I can't recall all of the story, but it seems that two lions were talking in the holding pens under the Roman Colosseum during the first century. Finally, one lion said to the other lion, "Aren't you just *fed up* with Christians?"

That punch line repeatedly came into focus recently in my mail and in my phone calls and personal encounters. Just this month I've seen, observed, and heard an unnerving number of Christians who say they are "fed up" with other Christians.

It's true that some Christians may seem to be one disappointment after another. They can be dishonest, disloyal, and even disagreeable. I may not even understand or agree with another's doctrine or theology.

But I'm not writing this to discuss how Christians have disappointed me. Rather, I want to point out at least three consequences of becoming "fed up" with other Christians.

First, I become a limited person. When I spend time judging the disappointing lives of other Christians, I am robbed of valuable time to concentrate on what God wants to do in *my* life. The

Pharisee who thanked God he wasn't like that "sinner" over there lost his potential for being the man God wanted him to be (Luke 18:11).

The act of focusing on the "failures" of other people limits what God wants to accomplish in *my own* life.

Next, I lose my joy. When I've just *had it* with Christians, I find myself in direct disobedience to one of Jesus' most important commands—to love one another (John 15:12). "If anyone says, 'I love God,' but keeps on hating his brother, he is a liar." (1 John 4:20). So, my joy gets very troubled or I lose it altogether. When my joy in Christ is gone, a vacancy is left in my soul. Soon moodiness and depression move in.

Finally, Satan has a good laugh. When I spend time commiserating with friends about how Christians have let me down, the background music I hear is Satan chuckling. He knows he can't erase my name from God's Book of Life, but he *can* keep my eyes on the failures of other Christians—and cause me to lose my purpose and direction.

If you've reached the *I'm-fed-up-with-Christians* stage, I pray God will restore to you *His* marvelous, luminous joy, and show you your own priceless potential in Him.

♥ *That's what He had to do with me today.*

♥

MAD AS A WET HEN

Experts tell us that anger, a difficult-to-deal-with-emotion, is triggered by four main causes:

1. Extreme fatigue—such as what a young mother with two children under four years of age experiences.

2. Extreme embarrassment—especially in front of friends, family, or in full view of strangers.

3. Extreme rejection—such as one parent (or both) never giving their child approval.

4. Extreme frustration—such as doing the very best job and then seeing everything go wrong.

Some seem to think that, as Christians, we should not show anger. I don't think that's true. Anger is a God-given emotion. It's how a Christian handles and controls anger that either causes or keeps him from sin.

We are told in the Book of Galatians that the fruits of the Spirit are love, joy, peace, self-control. . . . But, mind you, we must be walking in the Spirit in order for these fruits to be produced in our lives.

That brings me to the word *control*. I can control my *attitude* about anger, and disruptive thoughts if I choose to. It may mean getting up each day and deciding who's going to be in control of my life.

I can let my circumstances be in control and watch everything fall apart, or I can choose to ask the Holy Spirit to be in charge, thereby experiencing the fruit of His power. I'm not saying it's easy, but my emotional reactions can hurt myself and others if the Spirit isn't in control. So when I first feel the surge of anger, I need to:

1. Recognize what problem has brought the anger into focus (fatigue, embarrassment, rejection, or frustration).

2. Choose to depend on the Lord's Holy Spirit to help you control and handle anger. The Bible says, "Be ye angry, and sin not" (Ephesians 4:26, KJV). So evidently the emotion of anger in itself is not a sin. But to harm someone verbally, emotionally, or physically is.

I know that I will grow frustrated and angry from time to time, but if I'm trying to walk in the Spirit and choosing to let the Lord lead, He will give me the power to control the by-product of my emotional reaction.

One other word about anger. Since the emotion of anger causes many biochemical reactions, such as the rise of blood pressure, I need to redirect and rechannel the added pressure in some new positive way.

I've found that vacuuming every rug in the house releases much of my tension. But it gets rather funny when my daughter, Laurie, walks into my house and seeing the clean carpets asks, "Who are we mad at today?"

♥ *Lord, from time to time some of the factors which trigger anger will be present in my emotions. You, who made me and know all about me (Psalm 139), please help me to choose the right attitudes so your fruits of the spirit will be seen in my life.*

♥

HARD OF HEARING

Just yesterday I read some statistics which proved what I already knew: the noise level in my house is highest in the kitchen.

Much of my time as a wife and mother is spent in that noisy chamber and, because of the high decibel count, I'm sure I'm getting a little hard-of-hearing.

As I think of it, some of the most important decisions of my life have been prayed and pondered over as I leaned against the kitchen sink. The towel hanging beside the sink has been used for more than drying the dishes. For sure.

The children's big, bigger, and biggest questions have been asked in the kitchen while we did the dishes or later while *they* did the dishes or while fixing a snack.

Personally, while I've been in the kitchen, I've reminded the Lord about my need for His wisdom over and over again.

Today I prayed:

Lord, I think I've just figured out why You have to shout so loudly at me. I'm spiritually hard-of-hearing. The noise level of the tensions and problems here in my kitchen have dulled my sensitivity to Your voice.

My ears have grown accustomed to the din of
  families,
  freeways,
  working,
  cleaning,
  questions, and
  phones.

I think I need a hearing aid—one that's really turned up—or maybe I need a short time to withdraw from my kitchen and spiritually re-charge my batteries.

Otherwise, I'll miss the sound of
  a friend hurting,
  a daughter crying,
  a co-worker failing,
  a husband hurting, or
  a neighbor rejoicing.

Lord, I don't want to miss anything! But there's a tremendous amount of interference going on down here, so please wash the apathy of indifference out of the inner place of my soul, remove the air-hammer-voice of Satan, heal the infection of bitterness, and soothe the harshness of sounds with Your warm, fragrant balm of Gilead oil before I drown in this sea of ugly noise.

♥ *Dear Lord, it's only four words, but it takes a long time to memorize: "Be still and know." Please help me to let Your whisper come through. I don't want to miss anything!*

♥

TOTAL AMNESIA

Hal Lindsey, in his book *There's a New World Coming* (Vision House), talks about the forgetfulness of Christians. He says, "Christians suffer from short memories."

I think he is too soft on me, as a Christian. Too often I've been guilty of forgetting what God has done in the past. A current crisis hits, and I suffer—not from a "short memory"—but from total amnesia.

My crisis wipes out all memories of what God has done in the weeks and months behind me. Then, for weeks ahead, I stumble around in the fog of spiritual amnesia.

The presence of the Holy Spirit feels as if it has vanished from my life; my prayer and Bible study times are dry and unexciting experiences.

I was comforted this week as I realized that the Psalmist David suffered a bad attack of amnesia at least on one occasion. It came when he didn't see any evidence of God's power in his past life or in his present troubles. He accused God of forgetting him. He said, "Lord, why are You standing aloof and far away? Why do You hide when I need You the most?" (Psalm 10:1)

He later became even more direct: "How long will You forget me, Lord? Forever? How long will You look the other way when I am in need?" (Psalm 13:1)

What David needed to bring him out of his amnesia was a 29 cent notebook to record his prayer requests and God's answers.

Today I remembered *my* notebook. I flipped the pages back over two months of requests and answers. Why didn't I do this before? It astounded me because I'd forgotten what God has done. In forgetting how faithful God was to me in the past, I'd left myself wide open to the blows of my new crisis.

Maybe David did have some sort of notebook. I don't know. But something restored his memory, because he returned to his senses and said, "But I will always trust in You and in Your mercy and shall rejoice in Your salvation. I will sing to the Lord because He has blessed me so richly!" (Psalm 13: 5–6)

There it is! We know we will have hassles, stress, and crises (Jesus told us that), but let's not forget: God can be trusted. He heard us and worked in our lives in the past; He will work now, in the present, and out there in our tomorrows.

♥ *Please dear Lord, awake me from the sleep of amnesia and let me awaken to your wonderful ways!*

♥

THE GIFT OF WONDER

One of the most precious things my mother ever developed in me was the sense of wonder. She left me this rich gift as a part of my inheritance.

I guess all children are born with a sense of wonder, but to reach adulthood with it intact and fully matured is practically a miracle. I think my mother understood the wonder-factor about children and worked to develop mine.

I was in the second or third grade when I noticed a field of yellow dandelions on my way home from school one day. I waded into that glorious golden sea of sunshine, picked all the blossoms my hands could hold, and ran all the way home. Flinging open the front door I shouted, "Here, Mother, *these are for you!*"

At that moment, my mother was teaching a Bible study and our living room was filled with ladies from Dad's church. My announcement left her two obvious options: she could shush me up or develop my sense of wonder.

With a look of what can aptly be described as magnificent awe, she laid her books on the table, knelt down beside me, and took my gift.

"Oh, they are beautiful, beautiful, beautiful," she said over and over again. (She *could* have told me they were messy weeds.) "I love them because you gave them to me." (She *could* have given me a lecture on picking flowers on private property.) "I'm going to set them on our table for our centerpiece tonight." (She *could* have told me they'd never last the afternoon and, aside from drooping, would make my father sneeze.)

David, the psalmist, was never too old to be lost in the awe and wonder of really seeing things.

Someone else might have only seen a few straggly old cows here and there, but David wrote about God owning the cattle on a thousand hills (Psalm 50:10). Someone else might have had the same canopy of stars overhead night after night without ever being moved by their majesty, but David wrote:

"The heavens are telling the glory of God; they are a marvelous display of His craftsmanship. Day and night they keep on telling about God" (Psalm 19:1–2).

I think maybe, just maybe, someone took the time to develop the God-given trait of wonder in David, to expand it and to encourage it. Our world has been richer ever since because of his inspired sense of wonder.

♥ *Dear Lord, my sense of wonder can open the lenses in my eyes so that when I look at things I really see them. God, please keep me constantly reminded of my heritage of wonder as I train my own children and myself to see everything there is to see.*

♥

HOLY OR HECTIC?

By Saturday afternoon, my inner tension had built suffi-
ciently for me to stop and ask myself, *What's the matter?* Then I
remembered. *Tomorrow is Sunday!*

How awful! The day that was supposed to mean pleasant
things really meant horrible, hectic happenings to me. I knew
the routine well:

Sunday morning—usual headache, grumpy attitude.

Sunday noon—arguing adolescent siblings, burned roast.

Sunday afternoon—indigestion.

Sunday night—exhaustion.

I talked to the Lord about our Sundays and asked Him for a
plan. I felt I needed a good plan, one that would make Sunday
a day of physical and spiritual nourishment for the whole
family. I confess though, mostly I wanted a plan that would
help *me* avoid being physically and spiritually exhausted on
Monday.

The Lord started His plan with me. My usual Sunday morn-
ing practice was to stay in bed as long as I could. Of course,

that left everyone else rushed, disoriented, and without much breakfast. I decided to get up ahead of everyone else, fix a decent breakfast, and start the dinner roast. (I didn't care too much for the plan, but I decided I'd better try it anyway.)

The Lord seemed to remind me that, while Satan cannot take away our salvation, he certainly pressures us at our weakest points. My headache, for example, was at its worst just as I was singing in the choir. My stomach growled all through the sermon, making me even more grumpy. The trip home was punctuated by hungry, angry children wrestling in the back seat of the car.

I called a family conference the following Thursday night. I walked them trough a typical Sunday (not that anyone needed it) and I ended by telling them that from now on none of us were going to be robbed of what that great day should be. We talked about what each of us could do to help Sundays get off to the right start.

I promised to get up early, get breakfast, and start plans for dinner. My family promised to control their own grumpiness,and my kids said they'd try to keep from fighting.

The next Sunday came, and many, many Sundays have followed. Not all have been divinely perfect, but not a whole lot have been the old unpleasant, hectic-type either.

God began to heal me and my Sundays.

♥ *Dear Lord,I really appreciate the beautiful beatitude, "Happy are those who strive for peace—they shall be called the sons of God" (Matthew 5:9). Because I know when I begin to "strive for peace," You hear me and give me holy—yes even happy—Sundays.*

♥

THE THANKFUL LIST

It's Thanksgiving time again. I know it because everyone is wearing their "thankful" hat. My mailman, usually very quiet, admonished me this morning with, "Count your blessings." The ad on the billboard by the freeway read, *Put a little thanks into your life,* and a delivery man I'd never seen before called cheerily to me, "Happy Thanksgiving!" So all this has set me to wondering just what it is that I am thankful for.

If I were to write a list of the things I'm thankful for, I'd put down all the good things of life: loving relationships, great children, and the growth I've seen this year in our lives.

But as I look over my list, I wonder about the *difficult* things of the year. Should they be on the list too? The scriptures clearly reveal that we are to be thankful and grateful for *all* things.

My list does not include the pain and suffering I've had this year, yet in order for my patience to grow (the Epistle of James tells us) I need those problems, that pain, and the suffering. My list includes none of the past months' disappointment, yet isn't it true that exactly when my disappointment was greatest the Lord, through one of His children, was especially close and comforting to me? My list makes no mention of the irritating "thorn" in my life, yet that very thorn has made me, no, forced me to see myself and God by a clearer light.

I think of my delightful friend, Audrey Mieir, and her song "Don't Spare Me":

Don't spare me trouble if it will bring me close to Thee.
Don't spare me heartache, You bore a broken heart for me.
Don't spare me loneliness, for I recall Gethsemane.
Don't spare me anything that You endured for me.
*But give me strength to follow Thee.**

And I am reminded that the lyrics make it quite a Thanksgiving song. It is not easy to make out a list of heartaches, pain, and disappointments and then be thankful over it, yet the Old Testament prophet did such a thing when his list read:

"Even though the fig trees are all destroyed, and there is neither blossom left nor fruit . . . even if the flocks die in the fields and the cattle barns are empty, yet I will rejoice in the Lord; I will be happy in the God of my salvation" (Habakkuk 3:17–18).

The secret is in the fact that he did not make up his list of praise and thanksgiving by how he *felt* emotionally. He made it a matter of will. He, like the psalmist, says, "I will praise . . ." *That's* thanksgiving!

♥ *Dear Lord, I'm making out a new list.*

♥

A WHOLE MAN

During the Vietnam conflict, some of the most moving experiences I ever had were in connection with the dozen or more tours I made for the Chaplain's Division of the U.S. Army overseas. Singing and speaking in "open-wound" hospital wards was very difficult; yet those are the performances I cherish the most.

One day, after I finished singing in five wards in the military hospital at Camp Zama, Japan, before leaving, I went back to speak to one more patient. As I walked to his bed, I noticed the soldier had no visible wounds, and since it was an open wound ward, I started kidding him about his "taking up a bed when others needed it who were really sick."

Smiling, he let me go on for a bit and then he grew serious and explained, "Actually, Ma'am, the reason you don't see any wounds is because specialists are upstairs now deciding whether they will amputate both of my legs."

For a moment I couldn't breathe. I tried to recover some mental balance, and managing to pull myself together I asked, "Is that scary?"

"Yes, Ma'am, it is," he said slowly, "especially since I have an 18-month-old son I've never seen, and when I do see him I don't want to be cut off here" (he pointed to mid thighs). "I don't want him to see me as half a man—I want to be a *whole* man."

Squeezing his hand in mine, I asked him if I could pray. He said yes and shut his eyes. Then it hit me that I had no idea as to *what* I would pray. But in the next instant the Lord reminded me of something I'd heard. The Sunday before I left for the orient Dr. Cole had preached and quoted the phrase, "Man's greatest problem is his brokenness, and his greatest need is to be made whole." It was all I could hear in my head, so aloud I began, "O Lord, all day I've seen and talked with men who have no arms, no legs, and, some, no faces. I'll never forget the horror of it all, but far more tragic than missing limbs and faces is the man whose heart is fragmented—cut in half—or in desperate need of God's touch."

I continued praying, not for that young man's impending surgery, but for his heart to be made whole by the touch of Jesus so it could hold forgiveness, joy, and the presence of God. When I finished praying he startled me by yelling, "Wow! How did you know that's what I needed?" His face was absolutely shining. Then excitedly he called the chaplain over and said, "Go upstairs and tell them I'm ready for their verdict. I don't care what they've decided, I'm ready. I'm a *whole* man no matter *what*."

Months later, the hospital chaplain told me the doctors decided against amputating his legs and that the soldier went all over the hospital telling other wounded men about "being whole in the heart."

Many times since then when I've been all absorbed in what I might lose, what I might not get, or what I might miss, I'm reminded of that soldier.

♥ *Dear Lord, help me to recall that the real issue of my heart is its condition. Exchange my brokenness with your wholeness. And thank you for the lesson you gave me through that soldier at Camp Zama Hospital in the open-wound ward and wherever he is today—kiss him with your blessings.*

♥

WELCOME OR?

All day long I've been smiling over the humorous truth of a cartoon I saw. A little boy and his friend were looking down at the word *Welcome* on the doormat. Pointing to it, one boy said to the other, "That's the first thing I learned to read. It says, *'Wipe your feet!'*"

I thought about all the times we've said one thing, but communicated quite another.

Spoken: "Pick up your clothes; your room is a mess!"

Communicated: "You are so dumb! How long am I going to have to tell you these things?

Spoken: "Hello, how are you?"

Communicated: "I really don't have time to listen or care."

Spoken: "Darling, you do it *this* way."

Communicated: "Stupid!"

Since some claim that only seven percent of what we communicate is verbal, the rest lies in such things as our vocal pitch, inflections, and facial expression.

Once when I was concentrating on peeling potatoes, I suddenly realized that five-year-old Laurie was standing quite close to me, studying me seriously. Looking gravely into my eyes, she said, "Mother, are you happy to me?"

I bent down, hugged her, and reassured her of my love and then I realized that she was *reading my face.* I was frowning at those potatoes, and she took it personally.

How many times are we engrossed in our own problematic world to the point that our faces show no love or kindness? There comes a time in all our lives when we are held accountable for the expressions on our faces.

When we speak, we very often communicate something quite opposite from our words because we are not being honest. I don't mean we should just say whatever we feel, even if it tears down and destroys. Instead, we should ask God for an honest love for others. Then our kind words will come across that way.

We also need to back up our words with honest, Christ-like living, even on Mondays.

Have you ever watched a car with a bumper sticker that reads, *Smile, God loves you,* weave in and out of lanes and cut off other cars? I have, and thought, *I'm smiling because God loves me, but I'm not too sure God is smiling at the driver.* He was not backing up his sticker with honest, Christ-like behavior.

Back to my cartoon—perhaps it would be more honest if most doormats read: WIPE YOUR FEET—PLEASE?

♥ *Dear Lord, so often I'm tempted to speak before I think. . . . Slow my quick tongue so my heart and mind can catch up. There are enough hurts in the world without my adding to them.*

♥

TROPHY TIME

We live in an age that delights in giving awards. We have trophies for sports; prizes for literary and journalistic achievement; awards for medicine and science; Tony's, Emmy and Academy Awards for the arts; and on and on. In fact, we even have the man-, woman-, boy-, and girl-of-the-year awards. Nothing gives us more delight than giving awards—except possibly receiving them.

So I've drawn up my own list this year. And I now present the Joyce Landorf Heatherley Trophies . . .

To the girl who kept quiet at lunchtime when everyone else was freely giving her their critical opinions about a mutual friend. "A true friend is always loyal" (Proverbs 17:17).

To the woman who accepted the nomination to be her church's women's missionary president even though it scares her to death and she knows someone else could do a better job. "Let everyone be sure that he is doing his very best, for then he will have the personal satisfaction of work well done, and won't need to compare himself with someone else" (Galatians 6:4).

To the woman who turned down the same nomination because she felt she'd be spreading herself too thin over God's priorities for her life. "You made my body, Lord; now give me sense to heed Your laws" (Psalm 119:73).

To the man who illegally cut in front of me on the freeway and then, realizing his mistake, waved an apology. "A man who refuses to admit his mistakes can never be successful. But if he confesses and forsakes them, he gets another chance" (Proverbs 28:13).

To the woman who came to visit me while I was still in bed with the flu and didn't ask, "How are you?" but rather, "Which shall I clean first—the kitchen or the bathroom?" "Humility and reverence for the Lord will make you both wise and honored" (Proverbs 15:33).

To the person who has just learned he has terminal cancer but says, "I belong to the Lord. He will not take me home to Him one minute sooner or later than He wants to, so I'll just be ready."

"We try to live in such a way that no one will ever be offended or kept back from finding the Lord by the way we act, so that no one can find fault with us and blame it on the Lord. In fact, in everything we do we try to show that we are true ministers of God" (2 Corinthians 6:3–4).

♥ *But, the highest trophy of all goes to you, my readers, and to many others. I give you my love, respect, and admiration trophy! You earned it! And you deserve it! And as a wonderful older lady wrote me, "I love you . . . and it's all your fault!"*

♥

BACK TO THE VALLEY

After a fantastic morning of a spiritual retreat with over a thousand women in Arizona, a young mother of seven children opened her heart to me. "I'm so high right now," she said, "but I've been here before. What happens when I go home is that I come crashing down. How can I avoid the 'back to reality' letdown?"

I was reminded of the disciples who wanted to stay on the mountaintop with the Lord, but He led them gently down off the mountain and back to the valley of the nitty-gritty (Matthew 17).

Why is it so hard to come back down off the mountaintop and pick up living in the valley? Part of the difficulty lies in the fact that the people in the valley—at our house or at our job—have *not* been with you. They haven't heard what you heard and they haven't experienced the spiritual awakening; neither have they been touched like we have.

It's quite a cultural shock. We come bursting into our home or job with all kinds of terrific things to tell about and experiences to share, and we find nobody cares! Our children have had a field day wrecking our house, the washer broke, the baby-sitter didn't show up, your husband came down with the flu, and someone at work quit, leaving us with one pay check for two jobs. It's really only natural that the *very* last thing *anyone* wants to hear is "what a wonderful time I had at the retreat."

I remember a teenager whose life dramatically changed after he accepted Christ at camp one summer. He could hardly wait to get home to share the news with his parents. He ran into the house not looking where he was going and yelled, "Mom, Dad, guess what—I've become a Christian!"

His mother took one look at him and said, "You just dumped a ton of dirt on my clean floor! Go outside and get cleaned up."

The boy was utterly spun off his mountain. He crashed and bounced on the rocks in the valley below. It's no wonder that he didn't want to share any more of his mountaintop experiences at home. He had been devastated by his mother's remark.

After our mountaintop experiences it would be good to remember to make it a rule of thumb when we go home that if we share, it will not be show-and-tell time.

What it really should be, is *show* time. *Without telling, we need to show our family, our mate, our friends and co-workers that something has transpired.*

If we *tell* them, we may find they are an unwilling or preoccupied audience. Also, if we relate to what was funny or deeply moving, it may lose everything in the translation of it. Then we begin to suffer from the back-to-reality letdown and the snappy little voice of Satan down in the basement of our soul says, "See, you didn't have such a mountaintop experience after all. If you had, it certainly would have lasted longer."

Nonsense! The Lord led His disciples off the mountain and down into the valley because that's where they *lived*. That valley is the place we really mature, expand, and grow from what we saw and heard up on the mountaintop. The valley of living is where God puts His mountaintop experiences into real practical, everyday, nitty-gritty lessons.

When we get home from a mountaintop experience, we need to walk in the door, thank the husband, the babysitter (or whomever took charge), hug the messy children, cook them a good dinner, do whatever—but most of all, just tell them that we really love them and missed them. I think they'll be able to tell that something happened on the mountaintop and maybe, just maybe, someone will ask, "How was it?"

♥ *Dear Lord, going back to the valley is so scary. It's hard to be so vulnerable and besides, my expectations are always so high for others. As I go home, hold my hand, Lord, and help me, in the valley, to remember all the great and glorious things I learned up on that mountain.*

ABOUT THE AUTHOR

Joyce Landorf Heatherley is known nationwide as a uniquely gifted Christian communicator, able to convey Biblical principles with relevance, humor, compassion, and gentle conviction—in a way that speaks to the needs of men and women from all backgrounds. A best-selling author of both fiction and non-fiction, her 24 books include: MY BLUE BLANKET, THE INHERITANCE, IRREGULAR PEOPLE, RICHEST LADY IN TOWN, UNWORLD PEOPLE, MONDAY THROUGH SATURDAY, CHANGEPOINTS, SILENT SEPTEMBER, FRAGILE TIMES, HE BEGAN WITH EVE, FRAGRANCE OF BEAUTY, BALCONY PEOPLE, and her latest book, SPECIAL WORDS.

Joyce Landorf Heatherley is also an immensely popular speaker and conference leader. Recordings of her more popular talks, including BALCONY PEOPLE, IRREGULAR PEOPLE, MY BLUE BLANKET, and THE INHERITANCE are available on audio cassette, as are video tapes of CHANGEPOINTS, IRREGULAR PEOPLE, and UNWORLD PEOPLE. Her HIS STUBBORN LOVE film series, based on her nationally acclaimed seminars of the same name, was the recipient of the 1981 President's Award from the Christian Film Distributors Association.

Any speaking engagement requests or inquiries concerning Joyce Landorf Heatherley books, tapes, and films may be directed to 1-800-777-7949.

Visit our web site at: www.balconypublishing.com